Big Bird

Written by Jack Gabolinscy
Illustrated by Sarah Anderson

The big white bird flew through a cold world of
dark storm clouds, wild winds, thunder and lightning.
Day after day, it looked for a place to rest. It was
hungry. Its strong wings grew tired and its brave heart
grew weak.

2

Sometimes, the big bird's black eyes blinked closed and its wings stopped beating. It dropped down towards the wild waves. But, just before it hit the water, it woke up and flapped back up into the clouds. Lost, cold, hungry, tired, it flew bravely on.

Tony and Irene were walking home along the beach. "Look!" called Tony, pointing into the sky.

A white shape came out of the clouds. Like a sleek jet, it dived towards the beach. Its wing feathers ruffled as it tried to slow down. But it was too late. With a loud, honking cry it crashed onto the beach.

"It's an albatross," cried Irene, dashing along the sand. "It's hurt."

Hiss-honk! Hiss-honk! Hiss-honk! The big bird's long neck swayed like a snake as they came near. Its big, hooked beak pointed towards them. Irene rushed to pick up the sick bird.

"Watch out!" called Tony, but he was too late. The big bird hiss-honked and pecked at Irene.

"Yeoow!" She jumped back, holding her face. Blood was running from a cut below her eye.

Irene rubbed the cut. "Wow!" she said. "That hurt. You try. Maybe it will like you better."

"No way," said Tony. "I don't want a bung eye." He thought for a moment, then said, "I'll walk around it and pretend I'm going to catch it. While it's watching me, you sneak in and grab it from behind."

"I guess so..." said Irene.

Tony walked around the big bird. Irene stood still. Tony stepped closer, waving a dead puffer fish at it. "Are you ready?" he whispered to Irene.

"Yes," said Irene, nodding.

Tony crept closer. The bird's black eyes watched him. Irene reached her hands out.

"I'll count to three," whispered Tony.

"One...two...three!" But the bird was too quick for them. Before they even moved, its head shot out like a striking snake. **Crack!** Tony's puffer fish broke into a hundred pieces.

Crack! Irene jumped back, rubbing a sore hand. "Next time," she said, "I will hold the puffer fish and you can grab the bird."

"I've got a better idea," said Tony. "I'll run home and get Dad. He'll know what to do – he's a ranger."

Irene sat on a rock, dabbing her hand and cheek with salty water. "Don't be angry, Big Bird. We only want to help," she said.

Hiss-honk! The albatross bobbed its head up and down. **Hiss-honk!**

Dad and Tony came back in the ranger's truck with a big cardboard box.

Dad looked at Irene's face. "You were very lucky," he said. "You could have lost an eye. You should have known better than to try and touch it without me here!" He looked at the bird. "You're right. It is an albatross. It must have been caught in a storm. It's lost and tired. It needs to rest."

The big bird and Dad looked at each other. **Hiss-honk! Hiss-honk!** it went.

"It can't stay here," said Dad. "Dogs will attack it and people might annoy it. It needs rest and food. It's not sick enough to go to the animal hospital. We'll keep it at home until it recovers."

Dad got a blanket from the car. "You hold the box open," he told Irene and Tony. "I'll throw the blanket over the bird and catch it. When I put the bird in the box, you close it up quickly. OK?"

Dad held the blanket out. He walked up to the frightened bird. "Shhh, shhh!" he said. "I'm going to help you, big fella."

Hiss-honk! Hiss-honk!

Dad moved slowly. Closer... Closer... The bird lifted its head. It flapped its wings weakly.

"Shhh, shhh," Dad hushed as if he was putting a baby to sleep. Slowly, slowly. "Shhh, shhhh."

Suddenly, Dad threw the blanket. It sailed up over the bird. Dad jumped in and wrapped his arms around it. **Hiss-honk! Hiss-honk! Hiss-honk!** The angry bird hooted loudly, flapping its wings and pecking at the blanket.

"Open the box!" Dad yelled. The blanket was jumping about in his arms like a bag full of wriggling eels. **Hiss-honk! Hiss-honk! Hiss-honk!** Dad pushed the bird and blanket into the box, but the bird's head popped out. **Peck! Peck! Hiss-honk! Peck! Hiss-honk! Peck! Peck!**

"Close the lid! Close the lid!" shouted Dad. But, every time he pushed the bird's head in, it popped out again, hissing and pecking angrily.

At last, they got the head in and the lid down. The big bird hissed and honked and jumped about in the box. It pecked and scratched, but after a while it was quiet.

"Oww!" said Dad. There were red marks all over his hands, arms and neck. "It's got a sharp beak."

They took the big bird home and put it in the old cage. For the next few days, Irene and Tony fed it scraps of fish, meat and vegetables. It ate everything that they gave it and looked for more. It stopped being scared and angry. It fed from their hands and let them stroke its soft head. It walked around, stretching and flapping its wings. "It's getting stronger," said Dad. "It's nearly ready to go."

No one wanted Big Bird to go, but on Saturday Dad opened the cage door. "It will go when it's ready," he said.

Big Bird stepped out of the cage. It walked up to Tony and Irene and ate fish from their hands for the last time. Then it lifted its long wings and pointed its head into the wind.

"Please stay," wished Irene.

"Don't go," whispered Tony.

Big Bird ran into the wind. Its wide wings caught the air and it rose into the sky. Higher and higher it circled. Then, like a diving plane, it swooped down over their heads. **Hissss-hooooooonk!** It called goodbye and was gone.

Irene wiped her eyes. "Goodbye, Big Bird," she said.

Soon, Big Bird became a shining speck high over the ocean. No one moved or spoke.

At last, Dad put an arm around Tony and Irene. "Anyone want to come for a walk along the beach?"

Big Bird is a **Narrative**.

A **narrative** has an introduction. It tells . . .

- **who** the story is about (the characters)
- **where** the story happened
- **when** the story happened.

Introduction	
Who	
Where	
When	When Tony and Irene were walking on the beach.

A narrative has a **problem** and a **solution**.

Problem

Solution

Guide Notes

Title: Big Bird
Stage: Fluency

Text Form: Narrative
Approach: Guided Reading
Processes: Thinking Critically, Exploring Language, Processing Information
Written and Visual Focus: Illustrative Text

THINKING CRITICALLY
(sample questions)
- What do you think this story could be about? Look at the title and discuss.
- Look at the cover. What is happening to the bird?
- Look at pages 2 and 3. Why do you think the bird is flying through the storm?
- Look at pages 4 and 5. What do you think Tony and Irene should do about the bird? Why do you think that?
- Look at pages 8 and 9. What kind of work do you think a ranger does?
- Look at pages 12 and 13. Why do you think the bird is pecking at Dad and the kids?
- Look at pages 14 and 15. How do you think the bird feels about being in the box? How do you think the bird feels a few days later? Why do you think that?

EXPLORING LANGUAGE

Terminology
Spread, author and illustrator credits, imprint information, ISBN number

Vocabulary
Clarify: thunder, albatross, ranger, cage
Adjectives: *brave* heart, *sleek* jet, *bung* eye
Pronouns: she, you, I, me, he, him, them, we, her, it, its
Similes: its head shot out *like a striking snake*, jumping about in his arms *like a bag full of wriggling eels*
Focus the students' attention on **homonyms**, **antonyms** and **synonyms** if appropriate.